soliloquies
for trees

soliloquies for trees

gabriel seawall

Soliloquies for Trees

Copyright © 2024 by Gabriel Seawall
All rights reserved. No part of this book
may be reproduced or distributed in any
printed or electronic form without written
permission.

Library of Congress Control Number:
2025923285

ISBN: 979-8-9936356-0-6

Cover Art by:
Gabriel Seawall & Anze Ban V.

Independently Published
Seattle, WA

First Edition

COLLECTION

1 - songbird

2 - twine

3 - ocean

4 - nature

5 - impermanent things

6 - leaf

7 - scotland

8 - hike

9 - between

10 - droplet

11 - beauty

12 - love story

13 - villain

14 - reincarnated

16 - reunion

18 - laurels

20 - straight

21 - dawn

22 - imagination

24 - books

26 - imaginary lines

27 - piano

28 - skipping stones

30 - career day

31 - succubus	51 - shield
32 - the spider	52 - justice
34 - temperance	53 - flame
36 - hunger and heart	54 - flaws
38 - the warrior poet	55 - empty
40 - half	56 - midnight
41 - princes	58 - the clock
42 - greatness	59 - ambition
44 - wisdom	60 - the sailor
45 - canvas	61 - wildflower
46 - oath	62 - lighthouse
48 - self	64 - the grey
49 - royalty	65 - thorns
50 - war	66 - violets

for
> the wild thistle
> the smell of honey
> the you who inspires me
> to be more than I am

soliloquies
for trees

seawall

songbird
—

could you sing the song of sparrows
find harmony in chorus
could you touch a shared emotion
then dine upon the forest?

do you need to know the lyrics
to the hymn of rising suns
to grasp a song is still the same
when sung in other tongues?

we may not be fluent
in thrums behind the beak
but our ears can make the melody
and our hearts can touch the grief

in a world of song and flight
chords fall from wings above
in a world where tender people
still dine on mourning doves

soliloquies for trees

twine
—

we are suspended
not by thick rope
nor by tempered chain
but by a thousand thinning threads

alone so ordinary
alone so frail

we hold no reverence
for common twine

but you are made of millions
and from the strength of millions
these humble cords
allow us to fly

seawall

ocean
—

salt sprays on hewn lips
as the sea bellows below
a violence raw
the ocean's maw
titanic in its rage

high above the sea
the chop fades to ripples
deep within the depths
her roar fades to silence

only gods and fish can see
the ocean is calm
placid in its entirety
except a single wavering line

soliloquies for trees

nature
—

nature is the one place
I could spend all day
doing nothing in the slightest
and still end my day
content in the thought
I've wasted no time

seawall

impermanent things
—

baby bird in your hands
can you open them with ease?
are you brave enough to love
these impermanent things?

can you chase the dying breeze
or the fading night sky?
would you love them still more
if this were the last time?

will you fill your soul whole?
would you run amongst the trees?
if what followed was a hollow
which you'd never be free?

those who live life fully
expose themselves to loss
the joyous and the mournful
know the pain is worth the cost

leaf

how many seconds
have you spent looking
at a single leaf?

veins explode
into a thousand tributaries

the ridges
patterned against the lines of my hand

singular irreplaceable beauty

but awe is fleeting
and seconds later
it is torn to pieces by my fingers

my eyes glaze and I watch helplessly
as something remarkable disappears forever

there are a trillion leaves in the world
but I mourn the loss of one

seawall

scotland
—

jagged crags and misty moors

an indomitable wilderness
an indomitable will

weathered soft by the winds of time
a land tenacious and free
fallen peaceful
in a happy slumber

hike
—

the naive seek battle
against the mountain cold
taken by a pompous sense
that glory's found alone

for if you close your eyes
and listen to the trees
you'll feel a heartbeat fluttering
soft underneath your feet

this partner outlives memory
her sweet breath fills your lungs
without her gracious gifts
our conquest is undone

lean on her when weary
each handhold is a gift
with aid of earth and root
we breach heaven's abyss

lower you erode her
with every path you shape
holding hands beside the mother
in every step we take

seawall

between
—

in our search for meaning
many look to the beginning
many more look to the end
when every reason lies between

soliloquies for trees

droplet
—

rain patters on a tin roof
streaks across my window pane

life carries you away
a single droplet
in the torrent of rain

my eyes blur
and you slip beneath
softly tumbling
to marry the creek

to give pause is choice
in this warmth I reside
embolden my heart
to take step outside

and I would chase you through the rivers
and I would dive into the sea

for on occasion you meet souls
who touch you so deep
that farewell becomes a word
you never dare speak

seawall

beauty
—

a sunrise sets the sky on fire
painting the earth with crimson hue

pristine flakes descend from heaven
weightless diamonds atop the yew

morning light catches reflections
of grass adorned with beads of dew

white marbled cliffs hide secret gardens
where lavender begins to bloom

the night sky ebbs an endless sea
as stars and nettle spiral through

dull I am to their seduction
when first of all I witnessed you

love story

—

first light
first love
not as bright as day
yet we peer through sheltered eyes

for before love true
all loves seem true
we write memoirs in the shade

no stories speak
of second sunrise
more brilliant than the first

we bathe in light
and yet cannot see
how bright the sun can burst

do perfect sunsets
justify
our gluttony and cheating?

a happy ending
is after all
subject to who is reading

seawall

villain
—

to be a villain
is a warm and sheltered life
harm without self-harm

perhaps if I were
I could spend my nights dreaming
but sleep evades me

pained not by mistakes
but by my love for those harmed
silently I weep

bad enough to harm
but good enough to suffer
I am imperfect

but I choose to be
and the world wallows in pain
so good can endure

reincarnated

—

ancient scars faded
reincarnated
lump sum gold
for your children traded

freshly signed
and twice revived
a divine contract
for spools of twine

memoirs doctored
history wracked
these labyrinthian paths
lie charted and mapped

old trials conquered
coppers at price
but gods without script
rehearse classic vice

seawall

same poison
new cup
renaissance gone
you'll drown in these dreams
of dusk's brighter dawns

—

reunion

—

enjoy this secret love letter
to a younger me
you're the closest I'll ever be to my family

mistakes were made
when I still wore my father's name
I idolized the founding father
held in reverent fame

I failed everything I tried
by never speaking out
had my legacy dismantled
fed these inner doubts

spewed your disfigured views
behind a porcelain mask
reunited as men
I see my skin through the cracks

years of reverence for you
met with bigotry
easy to impress the youth as an absentee

seawall

generation late
finding rot in the family tree
I refuse to treat my own
how you miscarried me

—

soliloquies for trees

laurels
—

in search of genius
we sift through laurels
atop their niche
the worshiped few

as if the brain
and not the heart
creates the drive
that guides our view

even the best
are found in bramble
weaving wicker
with tired hands

desert urchins
form no wreaths
yet barren soil
sees roots expand

seawall

despite the peaks
beneath the sea
we search only
atop the crown

we've less concern
for mastery
than how beautifully
it is bound

—

soliloquies for trees

straight
—

the straightest line
with purpose true
surrounded by
a crooked few
convinced him that
his course was strange
that he alone
needed to change

seawall

dawn
—

the sun rises
not because good has prevailed
but because the opportunity to do good
has not yet been extinguished

imagination
—

can you paint an empty canvas
with colors never seen
of a sunset on a world
where the sky rips at the seams?

can your imagination weave
another living being
made entirely of pieces
you've never once conceived?

we shy away from truth
that what's buried deep inside
is the shadow of story
already told by time

we pioneer
on plains once settled
the same four chords
drawn line for line

seawall

here stolen thoughts
drink from the well
of lives once lived
by shared design

every curiosity
the mind can bend to shape
is invented from an image
that's far too commonplace

a daydream turns to prophecy
while the universe conceives
for it paints in all the colors
we were never born to see

—

books
—

the ink which falls
by happenstance
will outlive men
as nations lapse

but mighty libraries
while vast and timeless
are only timeless
from mortal eyes

the sky like clockwork
all things are lost
as the smell of paper
turns to that of dust

perhaps I collect books
because I empathize
with the mournful dreams
kept by tattered spines

seawall

for every page I save
thousands lost to time
if I save enough
will someone save mine?

perhaps I collect books
because I recognize
that I too am surely
another victim of time

—

soliloquies for trees

imaginary lines
—

born just south
of imaginary lines
does courage survive
where color is crime?

peel back the clothes
the folks
the scars
do you stand self-assured
when cast to the stars?

are my eyes still blue
at every branch of the tree?
or do they only reflect
the views I can see?

put forth the virtues
that make you most proud
and I'll flush out the poison
that wove your faith's shroud

seawall

piano
—

soft chords hang in the air
a solemn song from years ago
my hands remember
what my mind has lost
remorse forgotten
turned timeless sorrow
fingers fumble
and memories perish
as melodies tumble
off ivory cliffs

soliloquies for trees

skipping stones
—

we dance through time
like skipping stones
above the silent sound
afraid that if we linger long
the depths will pull us down

rocks shatter thin along the shore
with shards of every size
the share that fly great distances
are weathered flat by time

but novice hands make waste
and sink the smoothest stone
while steady send the rugged
beyond the distant shoal

life gifts me a lone pebble
only one to test the sea
and though I've skipped a million
this fear embraces me

seawall

for if I wait a moment more
the tide will ebb and flow
rounding out some crooked cleft
before I let her go

I'm thankful that on every beach
there's lots of stones to skip
for if I dwelt on one too long
I'd never sway my grip

—

career day
—

my child is proud of me on career day
my position is so unique
I've achieved a dream that few can reach
a view atop the peak

my child is proud of me on career day
I work late every night
the cost of fame is mighty steep
but wealth well worth the price

my child is proud of me on career day
I miss their every step
absent from the precious moments
because I overslept

my child is proud of me on career day
but I sometimes wish they weren't
the cost of that which they hold dear
is far too steep a toll

I wish my child were disappointed
that I had some boring job
where I could find the strength of spirit
to be the parent they deserve

succubus

—

guilt the apple for your hunger
fault the river for your thirst
succubus on every corner
to deflect blame when at your worst

soliloquies for trees

the spider
—

I danced amongst the fireflies
through summer nights
and tired eyes
sweet grass beneath my feet awry
passion wells like rain

a hollow spider watched in lust
and pondered schemes to gain my trust
with gentle mask
she went to ask
to join our tasks for gain

I thought not of my future dreams
of golden fans
or ballet themes
only of this fleeting scene
before I knew her fangs

the spider wove her silver web
attached we were at length by thread
while free I was
now lost in dread
a mannequin now hangs

seawall

the puppet master hurled her line
performances were realigned
dull delights
saw dwindled lights
and shillings on the stage

barefoot
I knew no restraint
scuffed shoes on
when I learned hate
now I tap in perfect paint
trapped inside a cage

beware she speaks but does not hear
beware temptations of career
beware she makes your kindness mere
and blames it on the change

my somber fate
it holds no riddle
spiders
merely living spindle
pity how these fires dwindle
and no one finds it strange

soliloquies for trees

temperance
—

a thousand fleeting whispers
make judgments in her stride
hollow taunts
from hollow trees
who know nothing of having feet

warily
but starry-eyed
she cranes her neck and gazes high
heeding not the prickled teeth
that start to itch
the skin they bite

oh temperance
shed your clothes
these senseless squawks
see patience probed
as rumours pass
through listless crows
hiding in the eaves

seawall

but apathy
tastes like venom to pride
and steels resolve
to squander her time
serpents coiled
and ready to strike
rotting in the dark

lured to the forest
she no longer saw the sky
but a ceiling
in good part
formed not by what she could
but by what men deemed she could not

in little time
she proved them wrong
but only once the storm has calmed
will she realize
that these shallow burs
were never worth
the years now gone

—

hunger and heart
—

generations of apathy
generations of death
detritus adrift in a viscous sea

we reach for dark plumes
and swallow them whole
a newborn finds latch
to sate starving soul

possessed now anew
this need becomes longing
an aim without end
to weather night's dawning

enter abundance
but the hunger lives on
so we forge greater gods
to sate hollow want

as war shrouds the earth
with misfortune abound
a candle lit faintly
sees wicks tightly wound

seawall

to resist fruits before us
the heart forms a blade
now thrust upon self
to sense other pains

for inside each being
lies both hunger and heart
but which impetus proves
it plays greater parts?

I prefer most a kindness
to pull us from dark
but caution the folk
who measure our stock

in sharing our strength
we gain closer to god
you mistake it for kindness
but the hunger lives on

—

soliloquies for trees

the warrior poet
—

barefoot in the forest
velvet moss between your toes
the pang of jagged earth
forges battle in your soul

those who embrace callouses
and raze the earth with blows
march a path too dimly lit
with rubble in their tow

though some are gripped with awe
for how the flower grows
and leave their senses supple
taking leisure in their stroll

poems are born from softness
and wars are born from stone
such forests will determine
if pen or sword you hone

seawall

warriors dream of peace
where poetry can bloom
poets dream of epics
where warriors stay true

most embrace a calling
with neither path complete
become the warrior poet
feel all beneath your feet

—

half
—

we are only good
at half of all things
likely less
if born amongst kings

but we choose to act
only where we thrive
hiding from the scars
that keep us alive

thus we live in a world
where the bee never stings
where we tell ourselves
we are good at all things

princes
—

we are all princes
anointed at birth
to forgotten kingdoms
equal in worth

greatness
—

in the vast sands of time
how few grains I find
that seek to weather me
into something more refined

dreaming of a self
both dauntless and free
within this time
we realized
that half our lives we sleep

mortal bodies hunger
in every waking hour
perpetual pursuit
eroding from our power

time gone
to stoke the fire
time gone
to tend the buds

it is in the fractures of life
we find fragments of time

seawall

stories from sanity
symphonies from sleep
it is no great wonder
why the great artist weeps

what a life indeed
must some people lease
to afford the time
to see greatness unleashed

—

wisdom
—

great minds tread soft
on silken shoes
like desert winds
traversing dunes

for wisdom is a nomad
there's weight to what you read
but nimble minds will always find
where better paths can lead

take heed with your ambition
minds cluttered close as sand
the wise need never learn
but only understand

seawall

canvas
—

born bare
left to wither and scar

we treasure most the promise
asleep in its chastity
which never dreams of waking

a thousand rolls of virgin parchment
never allowed to taste the stroke of pen

for we confuse unity with harmony
and stain the virtue
of every original painting
which never sought once to conform

oath
—

a sacred oath
a solemn promise
a pledge allegiance
a vow of silence

to dying comrades
to weeping mothers
to cults of purpose
to dreams of lovers

the vows you make
are curses carried
with fewer fatal
than made in mirror

loyalties sway
nations break
friends can die
and love can fade

seawall

there's an ounce of escape
in every oath
a bond to break
in every case

if self forsworn
I wish you wealth
for you'll find no pardon
disappointing yourself

—

soliloquies for trees

self

—

who am I but you
born under circumstances
to judge what you do

seawall

royalty
—

royalty is
fear of winter's wrath
and reverence for spring
when they bear the same name

soliloquies for trees

war
—

war is fought by men
allied through astonishing chance
that a thousand unrelated obstacles
have a common enemy

seawall

shield
—

may you wield the shield
in a world of swordsmen

for heavy choices
demand strength to match

when wounds outlive
the anger they're carved from

and blades are sheathed
to protect none but an edge

I remind the swordsman
hands clenched in fists

nothing else can be grasped
without loosing your grip

justice

—

a hooded man
they now call justice
once went by another name

in time he learned
to choose his victims
malice scarcely sought to change

seawall

flame
—

winter's toil
flushed and numb
frigid breath
and splintered lungs

beyond this glimpse
of rosen cheeks
our muscles heave
on shivered peaks

a howling maw
that shatters veins
my hands burnt raw
from labored pains

a cinder floats
on bleakest moor
our flesh marred black
but we endure

soliloquies for trees

flaws
—

no method lies beyond a fault
from castle walls and trebuchets
there are simply flaws you've chanced upon
and those you've yet to pay

seawall

empty
—

to know pain
is to find the presence of an empty bed
heavier than one full

midnight
—

the lullaby of life
a eulogy of light
it beckons from the deep
it beckons me asleep
honey from her lips
a song I can't resist

the strange weight of time
lies heavy on your eyes
and you drift into a world
of whispers and sighs
no strength left to fight
the maiden midnight

time to choose
a love embraced
or a shadow refused
her sunless affair
a welcome curse
suffocated still
by siren's verse

seawall

yet we kiss every night
my lady midnight
a dark compulsion
a darker barter
the weight of our sins
for equal hours

is she goddess of life
or death?
or maybe just time?
a heart beating steady
in the cold eternal brine

too much to do
and too little time
or perhaps in the end
just too little light
bound by life
none can elude
the lanternless lure
of maiden midnight

—

the clock

—

imprisoned in a pocket watch
the metronome beats
procession to my execution
unable to sleep

born to ink dried long before
composed of common themes
the last act of this chronicle
results in tragedy

cursed to count the days we bloom
fallen petals
measured breaths
we only number matters
to add meaning to their deaths

content with life
yet paralyzed
at break of dawn
yet out of time

seawall

ambition
—

he seeks the horizon
she seeks his approach
his greater ambition
will swallow them both

the sailor
—

a lonely sailor cast adrift
accused of crimes he never did
it matters not his heart of gold
for land will never see him old

seawall

wildflower
—

she was a wildflower
abloom on a hill
unrivaled in worth
now bound by a sill
I poured all I was
into that bouquet
despite all I gave
she withered away

lighthouse
—

the last lighthouse stands
alone forgotten cliffs
absence hangs as thick as fog

a hollow remnant
of watch abandoned
seeking purpose
with lifeless gaze

rubble at rest
not a groan in the breeze
the silence roars louder
than thundering seas

light splinters into dark
and pale beams careen
peeling back the veil
that's lurking underneath

wreckage reaching from abyss
fingers from the depths
painting blackened silhouettes
on water steeped in death

seawall

the lens of time uncracked but sallow
a vigil standing in the shallows
peels away like paint

a beacon lit bright
shines not on this empty world
for the dead haven't eyes
to see the light

—

soliloquies for trees

the grey
—

a fleck of black
adrift the dawn
limbo lost
on muted ponds
stillness unbroken
a shallow abyss
a hidden horizon
impervious mist
stone smoke rising
amnesia's haze
wetter than ash
but drier than rain
sodden and still
ripples on veil
where dim untouched
meets endless pale
a sallow shore
swallowed by grey
awaiting first light
to break open day

seawall

thorns
—

lost are the thorns and blood
the coven in their hallowed woods
fables carved on bark

we paint the withered rose
and bleach once wild groves
in shades of pastel green

these infants tame the thistle
their wounded hands betrayed
arranging barbed bouquets

a somber truth embraced
when ducklings still drown
atop these placid lakes

violets
—

death sings a voiceless climax
lie still and listen lilacs
no sympathy or guidance
for symphonies of violets
still ravaged but alive since
our savageries and violence
embrace this shallow silence
the severed strings of violins
deep down the grave reminds us
why flowers grow inside us

www.ingramcontent.com/pod-product-compliance
Lightning Source LLC
Chambersburg PA
CBHW030447100526
44580CB00002B/21